From Trails to Highways

by Stavros Diamandopoulous

HOUGHTON MIFFLIN HARCOURT
School Publishers

MAP CREDIT: XNR Productions

PHOTOGRAPHY CREDITS: **Cover** © Kevin Fleming/CORBIS. **1**: © Bettmann/CORBIS. **2**: Associated Press, **4**: The Granger Collection, NY. **5**: © The Gallery Collection/CORBIS. **8-9**: The Granger Collection, New York. **10**: The Granger Collection, NY. **11**: Silvia Otte/Getty Images. **13**: © Kevin Fleming/CORBIS. **14**: (t) © Maurizio Rellini/Grand Tour/CORBIS, (b) © Mike Randolph/ Masterfile. **Global**: (bkgd) © istockphoto.com/lijlexmom.

Printed in China

ISBN-10: 0-547-02173-9
ISBN-13: 978-0-547-02173-7

2 3 4 5 6 7 8 0940 18 17 16 15 14 13 12 11 10

Today, people who want to go from New York to Boston can get in a car and drive there in about four hours. Nobody thinks of it as a remarkable accomplishment. But when New York and Boston were just towns in the American colonies, traveling was much slower and harder. A trip between these two cities took several days instead of a few hours.

Today people travel on highways like this, but traveling was not always this easy or this fast.

SPEED LIMIT
65 MPH

In the 1600s and 1700s, most American colonies had no roads or paths to connect them. If American Indians lived nearby, you might find a narrow walking trail. But such trails were not easy to follow. The early American colonists hardly went anywhere because travel was so difficult.

Unlike the United States today, the early American colonies had only a few small towns and no roads to connect them.

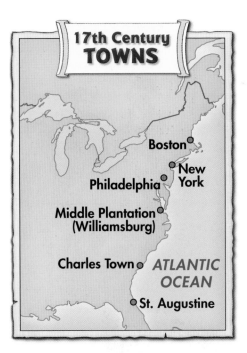

17th Century
TOWNS

Boston
New York
Philadelphia
Middle Plantation (Williamsburg)
Charles Town
ATLANTIC OCEAN
St. Augustine

The early colonies had no complex system of roads. There was no need for highways because automobiles, trucks, and buses did not exist. These inventions would not be around for a long time. The fastest form of transportation in the colonies was a horse. Even if a colonist was in a hurry, he or she could not go much more than a few miles in an hour.

When early colonists went somewhere, they walked or, if they were lucky, rode a horse.

American colonists preferred to travel and move large amounts of cargo by water. For this reason, the towns that grew most quickly were cities such as Boston or New York that were next to the ocean or big rivers. Ships took cargo and passengers all over the colonies. People also used small boats and canoes to travel on rivers and streams.

Most early colonial towns were ports, located on the Atlantic coast or on a big river.

As time passed, the colonial population grew, and so did American towns. More than 2,500 people lived in Philadelphia by 1701. Roads connected places within the town and connected Philadelphia to nearby farms. The early roads were nothing but dirt. Rain made them muddy and hard to walk or ride on. Later, surfaces composed of gravel helped to make roads easier to use.

Philadelphia was one of colonial America's biggest cities and one of the first to have real roads.

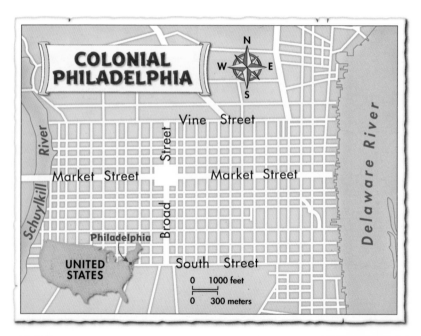

In 1654, a road connected Boston, Massachusetts, and Providence, Rhode Island. It was called the "Common Road." Later, the road went all the way to New York. People called it "The Shore Road." Then it was called "The Boston Post Road" because people used it to carry the "post"—the mail—from one city to the other. Today local traffic still uses the Post Road.

There were many post roads in the colonies.

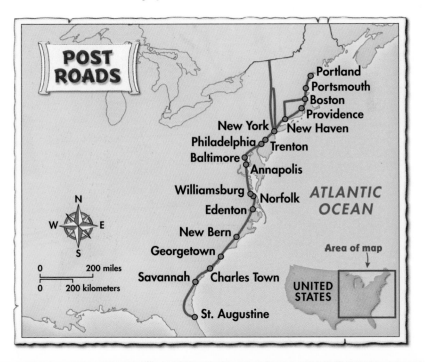

POST ROADS

Portland
Portsmouth
Boston
Providence
New York
New Haven
Philadelphia
Trenton
Baltimore
Annapolis
Williamsburg
Norfolk
Edenton
New Bern
Georgetown
Savannah
Charles Town
St. Augustine

ATLANTIC OCEAN

N
W — E
S

0   200 miles
0   200 kilometers

Area of map

UNITED STATES

By the early 1700s, people could take stagecoaches between towns. It was better than horseback—but not much. The coaches had no springs, so passengers had a bumpy ride. Coaches were pretty slow, too. Stagecoaches made trips in "stages." Coaches stopped each evening at inns, where passengers stayed overnight. A stagecoach took three days to go from Boston to New York.

Travel became easier in the late 1700s. A better-designed stagecoach had springs that softened bumps in the roads. This coach, called "the flying machine," could go faster than older coaches. As a result, it went from Boston to New York in only *two* days.

By the early 1700s, people could travel along the Boston Post Road on stagecoaches like this.

Carts drawn by horses or oxen carried cargo such as crops and manufactured goods in early colonial times. From the middle of the 1700s, Conestoga wagons became popular. They got their name from the Conestoga Valley in Pennsylvania, where they were first used. They were so heavy it took six or eight horses or oxen to pull them. But they could carry more than other wagons.

Wagons like this took pioneers westward in the 1700s and 1800s.

Some colonists made money by building roads and making people pay to use them. They called these roads "turnpikes." Wagons or coaches on a turnpike would find a pole (or "pike") blocking the way. They paid a toll, or a sum of money, and then a worker turned the pike so it was not in the way. Today there are modern turnpikes, where drivers pay tolls. The tolls pay for road repair.

Modern turnpikes are updates of those used in colonial times.

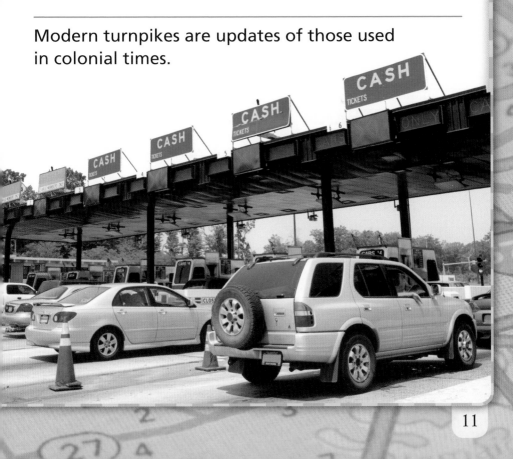

Most of the roads described in this book were in the northern and middle colonies. In the South, the population was smaller, and there were fewer towns. The southern colonies had fewer roads than the other colonies did. Virginia was the only southern colony where there was much road-building.

The southern colonies did not have as many roads as the northern colonies.

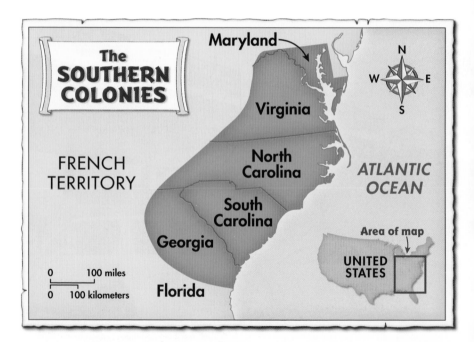

The
SOUTHERN
COLONIES

Maryland

Virginia

FRENCH TERRITORY

North Carolina

South Carolina

Georgia

Florida

ATLANTIC OCEAN

N
W   E
S

Area of map

UNITED STATES

0   100 miles
0   100 kilometers

Today the United States spreads across North America. There are national interstate highways, and every state has its own roads. Counties have networks of smaller streets. Almost all these roads, large or small, are well paved and smooth. Trips that once took days or even weeks to make now take only part of a day.

The modern United States road system covers the whole nation with highways and smaller streets.

America has changed a lot since the first colonists arrived hundreds of years ago. Colonists found no houses, stores, or other buildings, and no streets or cars or other vehicles. We need to remember what those colonists started with to appreciate what they were able to achieve.

Responding

✔ **TARGET SKILL** **Compare and Contrast**

How are colonial roads and modern roads alike? How are they different? Copy and complete the diagram below.

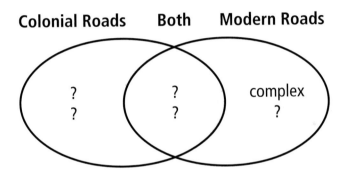

Colonial Roads   **Both**   **Modern Roads**

?
?

?
?

complex
?

Write About It

Text to World How did road-building help the country grow and change? Write a paragraph that expresses your opinion. Use opinion words and phrases to explain what you think.

 **TARGET VOCABULARY**

accomplishments	designed
achieve	inventions
amounts	remarkable
composed	result

EXPAND YOUR VOCABULARY

complex	toll
stagecoaches	transportation
system	turnpikes

TARGET SKILL **Compare and Contrast**
Tell how two things are alike or not.

TARGET STRATEGY **Visualize** Picture what
is happening as you read.

GENRE Informational text gives facts
about a topic.